A Chair's First 100 Days
a practical guide to the basics of board leadership

Tesse Akpeki, edited by Marta Maretich

Acknowledgements

Our thanks go to Emma King, Rebecca Forrester, Linda Laurance, Ade Sawyerr, and Peter Dyer. Their useful insights and comments have brought a practicality to this publication that makes it such a valuable resource. We are grateful for the support of the Home Office Active Community Directorate without which this publication would not have been possible. A big thanks goes to Marta Maretich who edited this publication and burnt the midnight oil with me as we both worked through so many drafts.

Published by NCVO Publications
National Council for Voluntary Organisations
Regent's Wharf, 8 All Saints Street, London N1 9RL

Designed by Philip Pestell, NCVO.
Printed by Skyline Limited.

Contents

Introduction

In our extensive work with the voluntary sector, NCVO has come to realise how important the board Chair is to the success of any organisation. The Chair guides activity in the boardroom, regulates governance processes, sets the tone for board/chief executive officer (CEO) relations and is, very often, the 'face' of the trustee board to the world. There is simply no more pivotal figure in the whole organisation than the Chair, not even the CEO.

It follows that the role is challenging: there is much to do and much rides on the personal qualities and skills of the individual. Yet, until now, there has been relatively little recognition of the need to support and develop voluntary sector Chairs. First-time Chairs – and our recent research shows that there are many of you out there – are particularly disadvantaged. Most new Chairs bring a deep commitment to the organisation but little of the necessary experience to do the job successfully. And because organisations have been slow to introduce proper training programmes for new Chairs, a high percentage take up the post without the benefit of any formal induction or handover process. The result is too often new Chairs who feel – and indeed are – poorly equipped to fulfil their duties.

In the absence of useful guidance, these dedicated individuals cope as best they can, but the going is tough. Left to learn their job on the hoof, often by a painful process of trial and error, they worry that they are failing the organisation. Some end up adopting practices that harm rather than help, others simply fail to live up to their leadership potential. A fair few just give up. If they stay, their role is often lonely and thankless. Many have no one with whom to share their concerns or from whom to seek support. Most have no idea where to obtain the further training that can help them succeed.

Help for new Chairs

NCVO sees a pressing need for more Chair support in organisations of all kinds, especially for first-time Chairs. As a step toward doing our part to meet this need, *A Chair's First 100 Days* provides a straightforward introduction designed to help new Chairs understand – and make the most of – their important role. Intended as a first resource for Chairs, the guide explains the role in clear, everyday language, giving an overview of the duties and responsibilities and offering valuable advice on where to go for more help and support.

Although aimed primarily at new Chairs or Chairs with limited experience, *A Chair's First 100 Days* is not only for Chairs – and not only for the first 100 days of tenure. It will also be a useful resource for those training, coaching and mentoring Chairs at any point in their development. Boards can use the guide as a benchmark when writing Chair job descriptions or launching a Chair recruitment drive. Organisations setting up Chair induction programmes will find the guide offers a convenient framework for structuring Chair information packages and induction activities. However, those who require detailed technical and legal information about the role of Chair should refer to NCVO's comprehensive *Good Trustee Guide*.

For more details of NCVO's publications go to www.ncvo-vol.org.uk/publications or call NCVO's HelpDesk on 0800 2 798 798.

Although NCVO is aware that the role of Chair differs considerably from organisation to organisation, we have tried to make this guide useful for the broadest possible audience. The legal requirements apply to most organisations regardless of size or type (when in doubt, check with the Charity Commission). The recommendations for good practice are drawn from our hands-on training experience, our research in the sector, and the findings of other agencies. These, too, should apply to most organisations, though in practice they may need to be adapted to suit your particular organisation, its structure and situation. As for terminology, we realise that both the leader of the trustee board and the top executive go by various names in different organisations. For the sake of convenience we've chosen *Chair* and *CEO* to identify these key players.

About the contents

What is a Chair and what does one do? sets out a basic description of the role of Chair, describing what personal qualities are needed and providing a list of typical duties. To raise awareness of the role of the Chair in your own organisation, *Different organisations, different responsibilities* gives a rundown of organisations at different points in the development cycle, describing the Chair's role in each.

Preparing to serve provides guidance on how to prepare to step into the role of Chair. Communication between the Chair-elect and the organisation is critical at this point and We offer a list of essential questions the Chair-to-be needs to ask about his or her role. *Nine key areas of knowledge* outlines the practical and factual information a Chair needs to know about the organisation in order to serve it effectively.

Continuing on a practical track, *Chairing effective meetings* provides a new Chair with some nuts-and-bolts guidance about how to plan and conduct good meetings. A special section on policy explains this critical area of board activity, showing how a Chair can contribute to the policymaking process and giving pointers on how to make effective policies. *Building healthy relationships* focuses on techniques for establishing fruitful working relationships with the trustees, the CEO, the staff and the public. Finally, *Preparing for succession* offers some guidance on how to handle the end of your tenure, securing the future of the organisation by providing a system for choosing your successor.

A starting point

At NCVO, we hope new Chairs and those training them will find *A Chair's First 100 Days* valuable as a tool for nurturing high quality leadership in the boardroom. An effective Chair contributes to making a productive, dynamic and engaged trustee board. By supporting the Chair in the early days of his or her tenure, the organisation lays the groundwork for good governance. This guide is one simple step in that process.

Portrait of a good Chair

The impact of a good Chair is first felt in the boardroom. Good chairing means that board meetings are well run. They start on time, end on time and follow a thoughtfully-prepared agenda. Trustees are able to discuss important issues – even engage in hot debate – yet the meeting stays on track thanks to the Chair's guiding hand. Strategic decisions get made, reports are filed on time, and every single trustee feels that he or she is making a difference by providing the organisation with the leadership it needs.

Beyond meetings, the good Chair empowers the board. Always alert to the needs and opinions of trustees, s/he listens carefully to what they have to say and tries to respond appropriately. By example and through the design of his/her agendas, the Chair fosters strategic, future-oriented thinking on the part of trustees. S/he helps bring about positive change by guiding them through development and training to improve governance practice. Leading the board as it sets up systems to regulate its own activities, s/he establishes sound recruitment practices for trustees, institutes board appraisal processes and puts in place communication systems to carry the board's voice to the rest of the organisation.

The good Chair's beneficial influence is felt far beyond the boardroom. S/he maintains amicable relations with the CEO, meeting regularly to discuss issues of strategic importance to the trustee board. Cordial but always professional, the Chair works with the CEO to keep the lines of communication open at all times. S/he leads the board as it carries out its management responsibilities toward the CEO, overseeing hiring, training, appraisal and the process of setting remuneration for the top executive. Always looking for ways to support and develop the CEO, the Chair offers positive and constructive feedback on behalf of the board and provides opportunities for further training.

With other staff the good Chair maintains friendly, respectful relations while always observing organisational protocols governing staff/trustee interactions. S/he serves as a point of contact with the trustee board but never encourages unrealistic expectations. With volunteers, members, service users and other stakeholders, too, s/he acts as an ambassador for the board. Here again the good Chair's ability to listen and observe comes to the fore. In public meetings, with the press and on government committees, the good Chair is sometimes called to act as the spokesperson for the organisation. When this happens, s/he makes sure s/he is well briefed and secure in her/his knowledge of organisational policy.

To help the organisation further, the good Chair remains alert for opportunities for positive publicity and useful networking. S/he keeps an eye out for potential trustees and Chairs of the future. Within the constraints of the Trustee Code of Conduct, s/he uses personal contacts and influence appropriately to help the organisation in any way possible. The good Chair may also choose to volunteer for the organisation in non-leadership activities. Lending a hand in fundraising or helping out with a programme, s/he finds, is a good way to gain first-hand experience of the challenges and opportunities facing the organisation.

What is a Chair and what does one do?

A Chair (short for Chairman, Chairwoman or Chairperson) is a trustee who is appointed by his or her fellow trustees to lead the board in its governance activities. He or she has a dual role as team member, having the same responsibilities as any trustee, and team leader, with the extra duties and responsibilities of leadership. The Chair often serves as the board's spokesperson outside the boardroom and is an important point of contact between the board and others, particularly the CEO. Yet the Chair is largely an agent of the board: overall leadership remains the shared responsibility of all trustees collectively.

Personal qualities

Being elected Chair is an honour that shows confidence in you on the part of your fellow trustees. You have a responsibility to uphold this trust in all you do. As the chosen leader of the central leadership body, your conduct sets an important example for other trustees and for the rest of the organisation. Integrity, openness, fairness, professionalism and a spirit of service are some of the key qualities needed to be an effective Chair. A sincere commitment to the organisation's mission is vital, as is an ability to listen – really listen – to the views of others.

A good Chair guides rather than controls the board. This can be a tricky balancing act that takes tact, diplomacy and good negotiating skills. The Chair must be able to lead, guiding the group as it makes necessary decisions. Later, he or she must stand behind those decisions even when that means taking flack or being called to answer for what the board has done. A clear understanding of the nature of group leadership plus a commitment to continuous learning helps meet these challenges.

Typical duties

In this special role, the appointed trustee serves the board by doing or overseeing much of the practical work that enables trustee boards to carry out governance work. Not all of this work has to be done by the Chair personally. Experienced Chairs find it efficient to delegate at least some routine tasks to trustees or officers. This is safe, provided the Chair monitors that tasks are carried out properly. Duties include:

- planning the annual schedule of board meetings
- setting meeting agendas
- leading meetings and facilitating discussion
- making sure decisions made by the board are communicated to the organisation for implementation
- representing the organisation at functions and meetings, acting as spokesperson when appropriate
- working alongside the CEO to maintain an overview of the organisation's activities
- leading the appraisal and review process for the CEO
- acting as a representative of the board on appointment and disciplinary panels.

Providing strategic leadership

Underlying the many duties of the Chair is one fundamental responsibility: to provide strategic leadership for the trustee board. But what is strategic leadership and how does a Chair provide it?

To understand this aspect of the Chair's role, you must first understand the role of the trustee board as a whole. It is the trustee board's function to provide strategic direction for the organisation. Strategic direction means guidance that helps the organisation face risks, meet challenges and, above all, plan for the future. A strategic outlook requires a focus on the long-term, the big issues. It is characterised by anticipation and foresight. Working as a group, the board considers where the organisation is, decides where it should go, and makes preparations (or requires them to be made) so that the organisation can reach its goals. Typically, trustees work closely with the CEO to fulfil these strategic obligations, but accountability for what happens in the organisation remains squarely with the board.

As leader of the board, the Chair has a key role in encouraging strategic activity in the boardroom. Such activity includes formal duties such as participating, with the CEO, in the creation of a strategic plan. But, for an engaged, fully effective board, strategic activity goes far beyond the formal. Ideally, everything done in the boardroom, every issue raised, every decision debated, will have a strategic value for the organisation.

The Chair is a pivotal figure in creating a boardroom culture that focuses on strategy. A strategically aware Chair uses his/her position to foster an atmosphere that supports strategic engagement on the part of the trustee board. Although it can take time to learn the ins and outs of all the issues that affect your organisation strategically, even a new Chair can set out to provide strategic leadership by:

- familiarising him/herself with the strategic plan and strategic issues
- cultivating a strategic outlook and strategic awareness
- creating meeting agendas geared to the strategic plan
- steering meeting debate toward the strategic
- leading board training and development exercises designed to improve strategic thinking.

Limits to authority

As Chair, you will undoubtedly be a very important figure in your organisation, but your authority is limited. When you take on this role, you must accept that:

- you have authority only as an appointee of the board, not as an individual
- you can act only in accordance with the wishes of the board as set out in the governing document
- your decisions and actions must be reported accurately and promptly to the board
- you must fulfil your other legal responsibilities as a trustee
- you must act in the best interests of the organisation at all times.

Different organisations, different responsibilities

In legal terms, the Chair's role is the same regardless of the nature of the organisation. In practice, however, the work of the Chair varies from organisation to organisation. Factors such as the organisational size, age and situation have a powerful impact on the way the Chair's role takes shape. The following are some profiles of the role of the Chair in organisations at different stages of development. Do you recognise your organisation in these descriptions?

New In a fledgling organisation, the Chair is often one of the founding members. He or she is involved in identifying a need and beginning the process of building an organisation to meet that need. Other founding members serve as trustees. Together, Chair and trustees set up the basic governing structures (the governing document, the mission statement) and register the organisation as a charity. Because the new organisation still has no staff, the Chair and trustees all pitch in to carry out the practical work, everything from licking stamps to driving the bus. There is often no clear distinction between the governance role of the Chair and the many duties he or she undertakes to get the organisation off the ground.

Growing The organisation is thriving and it's time to hire the first member of staff. It's also time for the founding Chair and trustees to begin moving out of their hands-on involvement and into their governance role. It can be a challenge for active board members to step aside and let others take over day-to-day operations, but their energy is better spent creating frameworks for new staff and providing strategic guidance for the organisation. The Chair plays a pivotal role by providing leadership to trustees and others as they make this necessary transition.

Mature The organisation is well established. Its maturity may be reflected in a bigger size or simply in a clearer focus and direction. Now the Chair spearheads the process of formalising and consolidating governance practices, creating policy, establishing cycles of strategic planning, instituting systems of performance review, trustee recruitment and training and so on. Chair and board turn their attention to the big issues that face their organisation, leaving its day-to-day operation to staff – with detailed policy guidance, of course.

Aging Things are slowing down. The original impetus behind the organisation may have died down, the public may have lost interest or the organisation itself may have lost its spark. The Chair needs to help the board keep the organisation on track, maintaining its vision and strategic aims through these doldrums, looking out for areas of risk, avoiding complacency.

Revitalised Chair and trustees work energetically to turn a lacklustre organisation around, revitalising its vision and mission. Working with staff, they help create strategies and programmes to pump new life into the old organisation. Alternatively, the Chair and board realise that it is time to wind things up, merge with another organisation or devolve some assets. Only 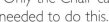 the trustee board can make these difficult, but sometimes necessary, strategic decisions. Only the Chair can provide the leadership needed to do this.

This specimen job description and person specification is specifically designed for the role of Chair.

Job description and person specification

Job title: Chair of _____

Job description

General responsibilities

- To ensure that the organisation complies with its governing document, charity law, company law and any other relevant legislation or regulations.
- To ensure that the organisation pursues its objects as defined in its governing document.
- To ensure the organisation applies its resources exclusively in pursuance of its objects (the charity must not spend money on activities which are not included in its own objects, no matter how worthwhile or charitable those activities are).
- To contribute actively to the board of trustees' role in giving firm strategic direction to the organisation, setting overall policy, defining goals and setting targets and evaluating performance against agreed targets.
- To safeguard the good name and values of the organisation.
- To ensure the effective and efficient administration of the organisation.
- To ensure the financial stability of the organisation.
- To protect and manage the property of the charity and to ensure the proper investment of the charity's funds.
- If the charity employs staff, to appoint the chief executive officer and monitor his/her performance.
- In addition to the above statutory duties, each trustee should use any specific skills, knowledge or experience they have to help the board of trustees reach sound decisions. This may involve scrutinising board papers, leading discussions, focusing on key issues, providing advice and guidance on new initiatives or on other issues in which the trustee has special expertise.

Additional duties of the Chair

- Planning the annual cycle of board meetings
- Setting agendas for board meetings
- Chairing and facilitating board meetings

- Giving direction to board policy-making
- Monitoring to ensure decisions taken at meetings are implemented
- Representing the organisation at functions, meetings and acting as a spokesperson as appropriate
- The Vice-Chair acts for the Chair when the Chair is not available and undertakes assignments at the request of the Chair

Where staff are employed:
- Liaising with the chief executive to keep an overview of the organisation's affairs and to provide support as appropriate
- Leading the process of appraising the performance of the chief executive officer
- Sitting on appointment and disciplinary panels
- Liaising with the chief executive officer to develop the board of trustees
- Bringing impartiality and objectivity to decision-making
- Facilitating change and addressing conflict within the board and within the organisation, liaising with the chief executive officer (if staff are employed) to achieve this

Person specification

General
- a commitment to the organisation
- a willingness to devote the necessary time and effort
- strategic vision
- independent judgement
- an ability to think creatively
- a willingness to speak their mind
- an understanding and acceptance of the legal duties, responsibilities and liabilities of trusteeship
- an ability to work effectively as a member of a team
- Nolan's[1] seven principles of public life; selflessness, integrity, objectivity, accountability, openness, honesty and leadership

Role of Chair
- leadership skills
- experience of committee work
- tact and diplomacy
- good communication and interpersonal skills
- impartiality, fairness and the ability to respect confidences

[1]Lord Nolan's Report of the Committee on Standards of Public Life Vol. 1 1995, HMSO

In most circumstances it would also be desirable for the Chair/Vice-Chair to have knowledge of the type of work undertaken by the organisation and a wider involvement with the voluntary sector and other networks.

Checklist

If you are recruiting a new Chair, has your board carried out a skills audit to identify the skills, experiences and qualities you are looking for? ☐

Are all trustees aware of the role of the Chair and other officer positions? ☐

A Chair is
- the chosen leader of the board
- first among equals
- obliged to carry out the board's wishes

A Chair isn't
- in control of the board
- free to act without board authorisation
- able to speak on behalf of the board without permission

A sample job description and person specification for a Chair can be downloaded at www.askNCVO.org.uk.

Preparing to serve

Now you begin the process of getting ready to take on a challenging new role. To be effective in the role of Chair, you will need to know some basic information about your role and about the organisation. A formal induction should cover many of these areas; make time for any induction activities your organisation offers. If your organisation doesn't provide an induction, you will have to actively seek out the information for yourself or enlist the help of those in the know. In any case, adopting the right attitude will help you as you go about learning the ropes.

Adopting the right attitude

Experienced Chairs agree: there is a lot for a new Chair to learn. Ask questions and don't be afraid to seem ignorant. Refer to this guide when you run into a new challenge or seek more detailed knowledge from other publications and from the agencies mentioned in the resources section (see page 31). Ask others in the organisation for help, or look further afield for assistance in the form of training and development. Remember, no one's perfect. Even when everything's going well, you won't always get it right. Still, your job is vitally important and your contribution is invaluable to the organisation. Do your best – and don't forget to enjoy it.

Clarifying expectations

The first thing to do when you are asked to take on the role of Chair is to make sure you understand what your organisation expects of you. This guide offers an overview of the role of Chair, but details will differ from organisation to organisation so be certain you understand the duties of the Chair in yours.

Although some organisations have a formal induction process for new Chairs, many do not. You should feel free to ask questions of the board, the previous Chair, the CEO – anyone – and expect to receive definitive answers. The discussion should go in both directions: as you form a picture of the organisation's expectations of you, you should take the opportunity to speak out about your own needs. The goal is to end up with a fairly accurate idea of the time and effort it will take to fulfil your new role. Review the following list of key questions to get an idea of the things you should be asking about.

What? There's no budget for Chair and trustee development!

Even the smallest organisation needs a board development budget. Money spent on training in governance, strategic thinking, self-appraisal or individual skills can have a powerful positive influence on board effectiveness. If you find your organisation lacks a board development budget, make establishing one your first act as board leader. You, the other trustees and the organisation all stand to benefit.

A new Chair's list of key questions

Meetings

- How many meetings per year must I chair? How long do meetings last?
- How much time will it take to prepare for meetings?
- How must I follow up after meetings? How much time will this take?
- Am I expected to chair any sub-committees or lead other groups?
- What support will I have? For example, is there a vice-chair or secretary to share my duties? Is there secretarial or administrative support?

Strategy

- What will my role be in the strategic planning process?
- What role will the trustee board play in strategic planning? How do you expect the Chair to support that role?
- What can I do to strengthen the overall strategic engagement of the trustee board?
- What issues will I need to focus on in the first phase of my leadership?

The CEO

- What are my responsibilities toward the chief executive officer?
- How can I best support and develop the CEO?

Further duties

- Will I have other responsibilities besides chairing board meetings and supporting the board? What are they?
- Does the organisation expect me to act as its spokesperson? When? With what groups?
- Does the organisation expect me to participate in fundraising activities? How?
- Does the organisation expect me to serve as its representative in any other capacity, such as acting on a governmental advisory committee or as part of a community group?

Development and support

- What is the budget for Chair and trustee development?
- Have the trustee board undergone any development or training recently? What was it? What was the outcome?
- Are there any important development activities planned for the trustee board in the near future?
- Will I have developmental support such as a mentor or a coach?

Practicalities

- To whom can I take my questions and concerns about my role?
- Will I receive expenses? Which ones? How do I apply for them?
- Will I be allowed to use organisational resources such as computers and photocopiers?
- How many hours per week does my total role require, realistically?

Look for help from...

Chair job descriptions and person specifications

Organisations should be able to provide new Chairs with up-to-date, detailed, written information about exactly what duties and responsibilities their role will entail. Job descriptions and person specifications can go a long way toward answering key questions. See the sample Chair job description and person specification on page 11.

The Board

Your fellow trustees should be ready and willing to talk about what they expect from their leader – and they should have given the matter enough thought to know the answers. They should also be prepared to listen to what you have to say and go some way toward meeting your expectations, too.

Your predecessor

The outgoing Chair has valuable lessons to teach. Some organisations carry out a handover process where the exiting Chair teaches the new Chair his or her role. Such arrangements can include a mentoring period or a longer apprenticeship of up to a year during which the Chair-to-be shadows the serving Chair to learn the ropes. Under the right circumstances, this can be an excellent way of ensuring continuity and keeping precious expertise from walking out the door. As Chair, consider adopting such practices for the benefit of your successor.

Development and support agencies

There's help out there: NCVO offers inductions for new Chairs that teach them fundamental skills in the context of their own organisation. It also offers a range of further training opportunities for Chairs at any stage of development. Charity Trustee Networks organises mentoring partnerships that give Chairs the opportunity to share their troubles with and learn from other Chairs. See the resources section (page 32) for contact details.

Things the organisation MUST do when appointing a new Chair:

- **Follow the proper procedures for election or appointment as set out in your governing document and other policies.**

- **If the Chair is new to the board, notify the Charity Commission in your annual report to them. If you are incorporated, notify Companies House, too.**

- **Advise your bank and make sure the new Chair is authorised to sign cheques and so on.**

- **Update organisational documents and letterheads to include the name of the new Chair.**

Nine key areas of knowledge

For a new Chair, knowing your own duties and responsibilities is the first step. The next is to get to know the organisation. Although it can take years to develop a complete understanding, it is never too early to start focusing on key areas and gathering the information you need to be an effective board leader.

1 *Who's who in the boardroom* Now is the time to get to know your fellow trustees if you haven't done so already. Learn their names, backgrounds and how they came to be on the board. Get acquainted with any board officers, such as the treasurer or secretary and find out the nature of their duties. Make a list of committees, their members, what they do and any important reporting dates. Some boards also have non-trustee advisors and advisory groups: learn about these, too.

2 *The shape of the organisation* Learn how your organisation is put together. Get to know how it's organised from the board on down including the CEO, department heads, programme directors and other staff members. Make sure you know about regional branches and their personnel as well as membership groups and any other organisations that work with yours as affiliates or partners.

3 *The organisation's current status* Get a clear sense of your organisation's current state of development. Is yours a new organisation or is it a mature one? Is it facing rapid growth or winding down some of its programmes? Is it contemplating a merger with another organisation? Factors such as these determine many of the leadership challenges that the trustee board – and the Chair – will face.

4 *Programme overview* Get an overall sense of the services and programmes your organisation runs. Find out which part of the organisation operates each programme, who directs it, and what group the programme is designed to serve. If your organisation has any service delivery contracts with the government, the local council or other agencies, then you need to know about these, too. Make field trips to meet personnel and see important programmes in action.

5 *Strategic activity* Your organisation has a strategic plan that sets out its objectives for the coming year, three years, or even five years. To lead the board effectively, you will need to be familiar with this plan and create meeting agendas around its key issues. Speak to the CEO about the existing strategic plan and make sure you understand what is expected of the board in terms of supporting it. Find out exactly what you and the board need to do to engage in the process of establishing the next strategic plan.

The board's strategic activity doesn't stop at the formal plan. As the main source of strategic guidance for the organisation, the board needs to maintain a focus on strategic issues – that is, issues that relate to the future of the organisation – at all times. As Chair, your attitude toward strategic concerns has a powerful influence. By honing your own strategic awareness and fostering strategic thinking among trustees during meetings, you will help the board realise its potential as an effective leadership body.

6 *Reporting schedules* By law, your organisation must file regular reports with the Charity Commission. Additionally, your governing document may require other reports at specific times. Get to know the reporting pattern for the year, so you will be able to plan meetings that return decisions in time to meet the deadlines.

7 *Milestones in the organisational calendar* The annual general meeting, the fundraising barbecue, the 25th anniversary of your founding, the training weekend for trustees: whatever the important dates for your organisation are, make sure you have them in your calendar.

8 *Finances* As Chair, you are not necessarily expected to be a financial wizard, but you do need to become familiar with how finances work for your organisation. The outgoing Chair, the CEO, the treasurer or the organisation's financial officer should be able to help you develop a sense of the financial situation. To be effective, you need to be able to read a balance sheet. Additionally, you should be familiar with:

- Operating costs
- Reserves
- Important projects that carry significant financial commitment
- Future commitments
- Sources of revenue such as money from fundraising, grants, contracts
- Factors that may change the financial outlook in the future
- Areas of risk

9 *Vital policies* Voluntary organisations are run according to a framework of written policies created by the trustee board. As Chair, you will be leading the board as they approve new polices and update old ones. By familiarising yourself with the existing policy framework, you will put yourself in a position to help the board carry out its duties effectively.

There are two types of policies a Chair needs to know about. The first are *organisational policies* – those policies set by the trustee board that govern activity in the organisation. These are broad, far-reaching policies that affect every part of the organisation and regulate its work. In preparation for your duties as Chair, get acquainted with existing organisational policies including:

- The governing document
- The human resources policy
- The financial policy
- The risk management policy
- The health and safety policy

The second kind of policies are board *operational policies*. These are policies written by the board, for the board, governing board activity (for example, how the board votes, how trustees enter items on the agenda, how trustee recruitment is carried out and so on). Board operational policies help boards work effectively. Creating them is an essential part of good governance practice. As board leader, it's the Chair's responsibility to make sure that board work is conducted according to these policies. Familiarity with them is a must.

Tip: For convenience, many organisations keep all their policies together in a policy book or policy manual – a simple ring-binder including all the policies in logical order. Such a book is invaluable to the Chair and the board as they work together to make policy.

For more information about creating and implementing policies, see NCVO's publication *Living Policy*. To order a copy visit www.ncvo-vol.org.uk/publications or call NCVO's HelpDesk on 0800 2 798 798.

Look for help from…

The trustee board

In your new role, you should be able to ask questions from any member of the trustee board. The exiting Chair has much to teach you. The board treasurer and secretary also hold valuable information, as do the heads of committees and those trustees with specialist knowledge.

The CEO

The CEO is a valuable resource. The interaction you share as you learn your job will form a basis for your future relations. Feel free to ask your CEO questions, but be respectful of his/her time. Avoid asking questions about things you can learn from reading reports or from induction materials. Focus on strategic issues, operational questions and matters that relate to the interaction between the board and the CEO. It's also important not to depend more on the CEO than you have to: you are aiming for independence and a relationship of equals (see CEO relations on page 27).

Other staff members

Other staff members such as the human resources specialist, the financial officer and the heads of departments should also be available to field your queries. Their know-how may provide useful insights. Be aware that many organisations have protocols covering interaction between board members and staff. You may need to clear your approach with your CEO before you contact a staff member directly. And, as with the CEO, don't make them drop everything just to help you. Schedule meetings at their convenience and try not to ask about things that you can find out for yourself.

Members of other boards

Chairs and trustees alike benefit from talking to other trustees in other organisations. By networking with your counterparts, you gain perspective on governance issues and learn new ways of coping with challenges. Seek out opportunities to meet and share information with other trustees through organisations like NCVO and Charity Trustee Networks.

Chairing effective meetings

Leading (or 'chairing') meetings is one of the main functions of the Chair. By performing this duty efficiently, the Chair makes it possible for the board carry out its vital work. The following are a few tips and pointers about how to lead meetings.

Good meeting basics

As anyone who's attended one knows, meetings are better when those in charge take care to observe a few common sense practices.

- Start and end meetings on time.
- Schedule meetings for times when most trustees can make it.
- Hold meetings in a place that is convenient, secure and accessible for all trustees.
- Provide transport and/or reimburse trustees for legitimate travel expenses.
- Offer refreshments.
- Schedule in breaks.
- Prepare the meeting room in advance providing supplies such as name tags, flip charts, overhead projectors, pens, paper and video equipment.
- Make sure seating is comfortable and that all participants can see, hear and be seen by the Chair.

For more advice on how to improve meetings, see
www.askNCVO-vol.org.uk.

Scheduling meetings and managing attendance

Attendance matters. It is part of the Chair's job to keep track of who shows and who doesn't. Take care to schedule meetings for times when the majority of trustees can make it. Don't insist that they take time off work, come at weekends, or sacrifice family commitments. Be flexible and accommodating. Be ready to change meeting dates and times if a majority wants it.

At the same time, have an attendance policy that makes expectations clear to trustees. Tactfully question trustees who fail to show up. Be prepared to remove trustees when they fail to meet their attendance obligations – but be sure you find out the real reasons why they don't come to meetings. An exit interview may uncover areas that need improvement.

Taking action between meetings

In normal circumstances, most board business can be taken care of during meetings. But what about when disaster strikes or the scandal breaks without warning? Every organisation needs a mechanism that will allow it to respond rapidly and decisively to a crisis without waiting for the board to convene.

To meet this need, many boards craft policies that give the Chair authority to call together a committee between meetings and take immediate decisions in the board's name. Sometimes called an executive action committee, such an emergency body might consist of the Chair, the CEO and one other officer: the policy specifies who can participate. Most policies require that the committee notify the board immediately of its decisions and that these decisions are ratified by the board at the earliest opportunity. As Chair, you should make sure your organisation has this protective policy in place long before it is needed.

Creating realistic agendas

Making meeting agendas – plans for what the group will do during the meeting – is one of the Chair's most important jobs.

- Agendas need to be set well before meetings and sent to trustees no less than seven working days in advance.
- There should be a clear-cut procedure for trustees and others to get items onto the agenda. Everyone should know what this procedure is and follow it.
- Agendas should be organised around important strategic issues – discuss these with the CEO and the outgoing Chair.
- Flag agenda items 'for discussion', 'for decision', or 'for information only'.
- Estimate the time it will take to discuss and vote on each item.
- Once the agenda is set, it's the Chair's responsibility to see to it that the group sticks to the plan. Make meaningful agendas and keep the group focused on them.

Distributing information

Don't use meeting time for distributing or reviewing information that can be given to trustees beforehand. Instead, distribute it well in advance – no less than seven working days before meetings. Make up packs containing the agenda plus reports, schedules and other relevant documents. Let trustees know how each piece of information relates to agenda items and whether they will be expected to discuss it, to vote on it or whether it's purely for their information.

Minuting meetings

All meetings should be minuted, that is, each topic of discussion noted with participant views and final decisions recorded. Appoint a recorder or secretary to make notes during the meeting and prepare the minutes afterwards. Trustees should receive a printed copy of minutes, preferably within 14 days of a meeting. Many organisations find email a convenient way to get copies of the minutes to trustees.

> **Tip:** Create a minute book – a simple ring binder to hold all the minutes. Leave it on the table for reference during meetings.

Facilitating discussion

Facilitating a discussion simply means keeping the debate on track, giving participants a chance to air their views and bringing the group to the point where they are able to make a decision. Facilitation is a key skill for Chairs.

A good facilitator:

- keeps to the agenda but leaves time for trustees to discuss issues
- gives all participants an opportunity to speak and be heard
- actively seeks the input of those reluctant to speak out
- does not allow any individual trustee or group to dominate the debate
- keeps the discussion focused and on track
- aims to conclude the discussion with a decisive vote
- records the vote or has it recorded.

Facilitation skills are useful in any role and indispensable to a Chair. Like any skills, it can be learned from watching experienced facilitators at work and by undergoing training such as that offered by NCVO and other agencies. For more information about facilitation training, contact NCVO's HelpDesk on 0800 2 798 798.

Managing committees

Most trustee boards have a number of committees. The complexity of the committee structure can pose a challenge for a new Chair. To help you get a grip, make a complete list of all existing committees. Note down their personnel, purpose, reporting dates and term limits. Don't forget to include non-board, or mixed committees, such as advisory committees, in your summary. Get to know the Chairs of key committees and learn what role they play in board decisionmaking.

When creating new committees, make sure that each one has a clear, written brief. The trustee board needs to discuss and ratify a committee brief by a majority vote. Such a brief should spell out:

- the aims of the committee
- its membership
- meeting and reporting dates
- provisions for budget and support
- any limitations on its activities
- its end date.

Producing policy

Policies are written statements, approved by the trustee board, stating how things will be done in the organisation. Board meetings are held to give trustees a chance to make policy. Chairs contribute to this process by helping set discussion topics, guiding and facilitating debate and bringing issues to a vote. Once a policy is approved by a majority of trustees, it's the Chair's responsibility to see to it that it is communicated to those who will implement it.

To be effective in the role of Chair, you will need to:
- familiarise yourself with existing organisational policies and board operational policies
- be prepared to communicate policy decisions to the right people in a timely fashion
- make a policy book – a ring binder that contains all the policies for the organisation – keep it up to date by adding new policies and removing obsolete ones.

The Chair can also have an influence by making sure new polices are well-crafted, with adequate provisions for implementation and review, and that existing polices are available for reference at all times. For more information on making policy, see NCVO's publication *Living Policy*.

Delegate for success

It's a common misconception among Chairs that they must do everything themselves. However, the Chair who tries to do it all burns out fast – and wastes valuable opportunities to involve other trustees in board support work. Wise Chairs call on the skills and abilities of their board members, delegating administrative tasks (like setting up the meeting room or sending out pre-meeting packs) and using their own time for more strategic purposes (like agenda setting and working with the CEO). By delegating – while monitoring effectively, of course – the Chair can do more for the board.

Policy pointers

- Policy should be clearly written in plain English.
- Check that new policies don't duplicate or contradict existing policies.
- Always include implementation provisions: instructions about who needs to put the policy into practice and by what date.
- Always include a review date when the board should consider the policy again.
- Don't forget to include monitoring criteria: how will the board know the policy is working?
- Put all new policies in the policy book and make sure every trustee gets a copy.
- Keep the policy book on the table during board meetings and use it as a reference.

Building healthy relationships

The Chair is a pivotal figure in any organisation. By building good relationships with trustees, with the CEO and with other stakeholders, the Chair helps ensure organisational effectiveness.

Working with trustees

In their relationship with trustees, Chairs should strive to live up to their role as board leader. Try to get to know every trustee by name. Set an example by always being fair, objective and respectful. Listen to their views. Take care to remain objective during board discussion and never try to dominate or impose your own will on the group. Keep in mind that you are there to serve the board, not the other way around. Let the group know that this is your intention.

However, an effective Chair is not subject to the board's every whim. The Chair best serves trustees when s/he maintains discipline and helps the group stay focused on their task. This can sometimes call for firmness. For example, when one trustee has held the floor too long, the Chair might intervene to let others have a chance to speak out.

Do your best to be tactful in such cases. Remember that trustees feel strongly about issues affecting the organisation and their opinions must be heard and valued. Help the group understand your reasons for intervening by reminding them of their higher purpose. If individual trustees have a bone to pick, make yourself available outside of meeting hours. Sometimes you can diffuse a situation simply by listening and affirming what someone has to say.

Honorary officers

Honorary board officers such as the secretary, treasurer and vice- or deputy- Chair can be of great help to a new Chair. By delegating some duties to these colleagues, you can share the burden of leadership and help the board run more efficiently. Developing a good working relationship with your 'team' is essential. But do make certain that you and the other officers are not perceived as a board within a board, an elect cabal that really runs things. Rather, strive for transparency and inclusivity, making it clear that all the officers serve the interests of the group as a whole. Make sure each role has an up-to-date job description to help clarify responsibilities and keep officers on track.

Developing the board

As Chair, you are responsible for helping the board improve its own practices. You will do this by assisting the group as it makes operational policies governing its own activity and by seeing to it that those policies are carried out (see Producing policy page 24). Additionally, you may be called upon to lead special exercises designed to help the board operate more effectively.

Board self-assessment Board self-assessment exercises are designed to help the board identify areas where it needs to improve its practice. Some boards administer their own self-assessments with the help of self-assessment guides such as that offered by NCVO. Others bring in consultants and trainers. In either case, the Chair normally coordinates the process. Chairs should encourage their boards to undertake these exercises, especially when there are problems in the boardroom or between the board and the CEO.

Trustee appraisal As part of their effort to improve board effectiveness, many organisations appraise the performance of individual trustees. The Chair plays an important role in administering the appraisal, analysing the results, giving feedback and setting goals for trustee development.

Board appraisal of the Chair Feedback from the board can be useful in targeting areas where the Chair needs support or training. One approach, adopted by Charity Trustee Networks, is for the deputy chair to informally speak to each trustee about the Chair's performance and then feed this back in a one-to-one session with the Chair.

Chair self-appraisal Chairs may be asked to carry out a self-appraisal exercise in order to identify development needs. Such exercises provide an opportunity to set personal development goals and seek further support and training.

Working with the CEO

The quality of the relationship between the board and the CEO plays a role in the success of the organisation. As head of the board, the Chair is an important liaison with the top executive. Getting that relationship right can go a long way toward helping the organisation function effectively.

The CEO/board relationship To get your relationship with the top executive right you – and the rest of the board – need to understand the true nature of your responsibilities toward the CEO. In brief, the trustee board as a group is the CEO's manager and boss. Like any good manager, the group must carry out certain duties regarding its employee. The Chair, as their leader, must guide the board as it:

- develops the job description and person specification for the CEO
- determines the levels of CEO pay and other remuneration (benefits, bonuses, etc)
- hires the CEO
- supports the CEO as he/she carries out organisational work
- offers him/her opportunities for training and development
- regularly assesses him/her
- disciplines and dismisses him/her when necessary.

The CEO/Chair relationship As board leader and spokesperson for the group, the Chair acts as a point of contact between the board and its CEO. This often means that the CEO and Chair work together on a regular basis. The Chair conveys board decisions, new policies and questions to the CEO from the board. Equally, s/he acts as a conduit for important information from the CEO to the board.

This sounds straightforward, but in practice it can be difficult to find the right level for CEO/Chair relations. If they are too distant, communication breaks down, sometimes giving rise to hostility. If they are too cosy, objectivity and independence suffer. Healthy CEO/Chair relations are characterised by:

- mutual trust and respect
- correct knowledge of CEO and board roles
- realistic expectations on both sides
- regular meetings to share information
- a focus on strategic issues
- a supportive attitude on the part of the Chair.

For a new Chair, it can be a challenge to feel confident when meeting with the CEO. In the beginning, it's common for recent appointees to lean on the top executive as they learn their new role, depending on him or her to provide information and a sense of direction. This is normal, but every Chair should strive to develop his or her knowledge of the organisation as time goes on. Eventually, you will have know-how to think and act independently – and so fulfil your duty to both the trustee board and to the CEO completely.

Other relationships

Staff

The Chair can provide a useful point of contact between the board and staff other than the CEO, fostering understanding of the board's contribution to the organisation. However, the Chair should always observe organisational procedures when dealing with staff.

- Establish a clear policy that spells out how the Chair and other board members should communicate with staff members.
- Never go directly to staff members with problems or concerns that the CEO should hear first.
- When staff approach with complaints or concerns, politely suggest that they go through the proper channels.
- Never gossip or break a confidence with staff – it undermines trust and weakens authority.
- Only use staff time and resources with board authorisation and staff agreement.
- Respect staff commitments: don't expect them to drop everything to help you.

Public

The Chair is often called upon to represent the organisation in public. As the 'face of the trustee board' you may find yourself addressing community groups, members of the media, service users, funders or government agencies. In this role, you can do a lot of good for your organisation, provided you observe some basic rules.

- Familiarise yourself with the policy that governs how board members, including the Chair, should deal with the media and public.
- Only speak on behalf of the organisation with proper authorisation from the board.
- Before speaking, be certain that you are fully briefed. Your remarks must be in line with official organisational policy.
- It may be dangerous to make statements when you haven't been briefed or aren't sure you have authorisation. When in doubt, say nothing.
- If you lack experience with speaking in public, ask an experienced board or staff member for coaching or suggest that the organisation foot the bill for training.

Preparing for succession

As you take up your duties as a Chair, it may seem far too early to think about the day you'll lay them down, but for the sake of your organisation, you must. Whatever your experience of the first 100 days of Chair service, good or bad, you will have gained valuable insights into how your organisation could do it better next time. Then, no Chair should approach the end of his/her term without a clear sense of who will take his/her place.

Trustee boards need to set systems in place for recruiting, training and inducting new Chairs so that succession is smooth and seamless. Every board needs:

- a transparent process for selecting a new Chair that begins well before the serving Chair is scheduled to leave
- a Chair job description and person specification
- a comprehensive induction programme for Chairs
- a training budget for Chairs
- a support mechanism, such as a peer network, for Chairs.

The Chair can play a key role in the process of establishing good practices for recruiting, training and supporting Chairs in years to come. By putting these provisions in place, you will leave a lasting legacy that will benefit the organisation long after you've stepped down.

NCVO

Regent's Wharf
8 All Saints Street
London N1 9RL
HelpDesk: 0800 2 798 798
(textphone 0800 01 88 111)
Switchboard: 020 7713 6161
Fax: 020 7713 6300
Website: www.ncvo-vol.org.uk or
www.askncvo.org.uk
Email: ncvo@ncvo-vol.org.uk

The National Council for Voluntary Organisations
is the umbrella body for the voluntary sector
in England.

NCVO's Trustee and Governance Team

NCVO's Trustee and Governance Team provides a
range of services to trustees and trustee boards,
with special services available for Chairs including
masterclasses, publications, online resources,
information and signposting.

Visit www.ncvo-vol.org.uk/governance for more
information or email trustee.enquiries@ncvo-
vol.org.uk

NCVO's Barclays Leadership programme

The NCVO Leadership Programme is a unique
personalised development programme designed to
help voluntary sector leaders perform more
effectively. Supported by Barclays PLC, the NCVO
Leadership Programme for Chairs and Chief
Executives offers a range of training options to
meet diverse needs. To join, email the Trustee and
Governance Team at trustee.enquiries@ncvo-
vol.org.uk, phone the NCVO HelpDesk on 0800 2
798 798, or write to us at our address above.

NCVO and CEDR

NCVO, in partnership with CEDR (the Centre for
Effective Dispute Resolution), offer a mediation
service for the voluntary sector. Please contact the
NCVO HelpDesk on 0800 2 798 798 as a first
point of contact.

Resources (A-Z):

Advisory, Conciliation and Arbitration Service (acas)
www.acas.org.uk
08457 47 47 47
Acas aims to improve organisations and working life through better employment relations.

Association of Chief Executives of Voluntary Organisations (acevo)
www.acevo.org.uk
0845 345 8481
Acevo represent third sector leaders and provide them with support, advice and development opportunities.

American Society of Association Executives (ASAE)
www.asaenet.org
Based in Washington, ASAE is the largest organisation of association executives and industry suppliers in the world. ASAE also serves as the international secretariat of the Global Forum of Societies of Association Executives, a global network for the association management profession worldwide.

Action with Communities in Rural England (ACRE)
www.acre.org.uk
01285 653477
ACRE is a national charity whose purpose is to support sustainable rural community development.

bassac
www.bassac.org.uk
020 7735 1075
The British Association of Settlements and Social Action Centres is a membership network of multi-purpose community organisations.
bassac represents its diverse members at a national level and offers them strategic support.

Black Training and Enterprise Group (BTEG)
www.bteg.co.uk
020 7713 6161
BTEG's core aim is to achieve measurable improvements for black people nationally, in four key areas:

- Employment
- Economic Regeneration
- Education
- Enterprise

BTEG strives to achieve these core aims through a range of lobbying and support activities. This involves working with black communities, organisations and businesses involved in regeneration activities as well as with statutory agencies that develop or influence policy in the above areas.

BoardSource
www.boardsource.org
BoardSource, formerly the National Center for Nonprofit Boards is based in America. It is a resource for practical information, tools and best practices, training, and leadership development for board members of nonprofit organisations worldwide.

Board Builders
www.boardbuilders.com
Board Builders is a company, based in America but which works internationally, dedicated to helping non-profits reach a higher level of success, and to help board and staff achieve greater joy in their work.

Charities Aid Foundation (CAF)
www.cafonline.org
CAF is an international non-governmental organisation providing specialist financial services to charities and their supporters

Capita Learning and Development
www.capita-ld.co.uk
0870 400 1000
Capita learning and development – previously part of The Industrial Society

Cass Business School, City University, London
www.cass.city.ac.uk
020 7040 8600
Offering a range of qualifications relevant to voluntary sector leaders.

Centre for Effective Dispute Resolution (CEDR)
www.cedr.co.uk
020 7536 6000
CEDR's mission is to encourage and develop mediation and other cost-effective dispute resolution and prevention techniques.

Charity Finance Directors' Group (CFDG)
www.cfdg.org.uk
020 7793 1400
The Charity Finance Directors' Group is a membership organisation set up in 1987 and specialises in helping charities to manage their accounting, taxation, audit and other finance related functions.

Charities Evaluation Services (CES)
www.ces-vol.org.uk
020 7713 5722
CES helps members of voluntary and community organisations to develop their own approaches to enhancing the quality of their services.

Charity Commission
www.charitycommission.gov.uk
0870 333 0123
The Charity Commission is established by law as the regulator and registrar for charities in England and Wales.

Charity Trustee Networks (CTN)
www.trusteenetworks.org.uk
01482 682252
Charity Trustee Networks helps set up and provides support to networks of charity trustees

Companies House
www.companieshouse.gov.uk
0870 33 33 636
Companies House incorporates and dissolves limited companies; examines and stores company information delivered under the Companies Act and related legislation; and makes this information available to the public.

Directory for Social Change (DSC)
www.dsc.org.uk
020 7391 4800 (London Office)
0151 708 0117 (Liverpool Office)
DSC help voluntary and community organisations to thrive through advice on: how to raise the money they need; how to manage their resources to maximum effect; how to influence the right people; what their rights and responsibilities are and how to plan and develop for the future.

Ethnic Minority Foundation (EMF)
www.ethnicminorityfund.org.uk
0800 652 0390
The Ethnic Minority Foundation (EMF) is committed to extending opportunities to people from ethnic minority communities throughout the UK.

Foundation for Good Governance
www.governance-works.org.uk
0191 232 6942
Foundation for Good Governance: works with boards to raise standards and improve practice; increases understanding of governance by research and shares models of good governance. See also 'Governance Works'.

Governance Institute
www.governanceinstitute.com
Based in America, the Governance Institute conducts research studies, tracks healthcare industry trends, and showcases the best practices of leading healthcare boards across the country.

Governance Works
www.governance-works.org.uk
0191 232 6942

Independent Sector
www.independentsector.org
Based in America, Independent Sector is committed to strengthening, empowering, and partnering with nonprofit and philanthropic organisations in their work on behalf of the public good.

Institute of Chartered Secretaries and Administrators (ICSA)
www.icsa.org.uk
020 7580 4741
ICSA is the professional body for Chartered Secretaries. A Chartered Secretary is qualified in company law, accounting, corporate governance, administration, company secretarial practice and management.

Institute of Chartered Accountants in England and Wales
www.icaew.org.uk
020 7920 8100
The Institute of Chartered Accountants in England and Wales is the largest professional accountancy body in Europe.

Institute of Fundraising
www.institute-of-fundraising.org.uk
020 7627 3436
The Institute of Fundraising promotes the highest standards of fundraising practice.

The King's Fund
www.kingsfund.org.uk
020 7307 2582
Education Leadership Development at the King's Fund runs a wide range of courses to help managers and health professionals to develop leadership skills.

The Management Centre
www.managementcentre.co.uk
020 7978 1516
The Management Centre run management and fundraising training programmes all over the UK and overseas. It also offers management and fundraising consultancy services.

McKinsey & Company
www.mckinsey.com
McKinsey offer free registration for an email update service for a range of topics.

National Association of Councils for Voluntary Service (NACVS)
www.nacvs.org.uk
0114 278 6636
NACVS is the network of over 300 Councils for Voluntary Service (CVS) throughout England.

NHS Leadership Centre
www.modern.nhs.uk
0845 600 0700
The NHS Leadership Centre was established in 2001 to promote leadership development across the service.

Nonprofit Governance and Management Centre
www.governance.com.au
Based in Australia, the Nonprofit Governance and Management Centre have a firm commitment to quality management in the nonprofit sector which they believe starts with effective governance.

Open University Business School
www.open.ac.uk/oubs
08700 100311
The Open University Business School is the largest business school in Europe and the largest MBA provider in the world

Roffey Park
www.roffeypark.com
01293 854 059
Roffey Park offers executive education, with a focus on leadership, people management, personal effectiveness, human resources and organisational development.

Sandy Adirondack
www.sandy-a.co.uk
020 7232 0726
Sandy Adirondack is a freelance management consultant and trainer working exclusively in the voluntary/not-for-profit sector.

Voluntary Sector National Training Organisation (VSNTO)
www.voluntarysectorskills.org.uk
020 7713 6161
The Voluntary Sector National Training Organisation (VSNTO) supports workforce learning and development for paid staff, volunteers, management committee members and trustees within the voluntary and community sectors.

The Work Foundation (previously part of The Industrial Society)
www.theworkfoundation.com
0870 165 6700
The Work Foundation exists to inspire and deliver improvements to performance through improving the quality of working life. Previously part of The Industrial Society.